ATLAS of
Southwest
and Central
Asia

by Felicia Law

PICTURE WINDOW BOOKS
Minneapolis, Minnesota

First American edition published in 2008 by
Picture Window Books
151 Good Counsel Drive
P.O. Box 669
Mankato, MN 56002-0669
877-845-8392
www.capstonepub.com

Editor: Jill Kalz
Designer: Hilary Wacholz
Page Production: Melissa Kes
Art Director: Nathan Gassman
Associate Managing Editor: Christianne Jones
Content Adviser: Lisa Thornquist, Ph.D., Geography
Cartographer: XNR Productions, Inc. (13, 15, 17, 19)

Editor and Compiler: Felicia Law
Research: Trevor Glover
Factual Researcher: Joe Josephs
Designers: Fanny Masters & Maia Terry
Picture Researcher: Diana Morris
Illustrators: Rebecca Elliott, Ali Lodge, and Q2 Media
Maps: Geo-Innovations UK

All books published by Picture Window Books
are manufactured with paper containing at least
10 percent post-consumer waste.

Law, Felicia.
Atlas of Southwest and Central Asia / by Felicia Law. – Minneapolis, MN :
Picture Window Books, 2008.
32 p. : col. ill., col. maps ; cm. – (Picture Window Books world atlases).
2-4
2-4.
Includes index and glossary.
ISBN 978-1-4048-3884-0 (library binding)
ISBN 978-1-4048-3892-5 (paperback)
1. Maps – Juvenile literature. 2. Asia – Geography – Juvenile literature. 3. Asia – Maps
for children.
DS5.92   915 REF
                                                  DLC

Photo Credits:
Age Fotostock/Superstock: 21tl; Kharidehal Abhirama Ashwin/Shutterstock: 23tr, Yann Arthus-Bertrand/Corbis: 10bl, Joseph Calev/Shutterstock:
18bl; Dinodia: 21cr; Jeff Dozier: 12tr; Xavier Eichaker/Bios/Still Pictures: 8bl; Eye Ubiquitous/Corbis: 23cr, Gustavo Fadel/Shutterstock: 25b; Free
Agents Ltd/Corbis: 9b; Blaine Harrington III/Corbis: 6r; Baldev Kapoor/Sygma/Corbis: 26tr, David Keaton/Corbis: 28-29, Kurt/Dreamstime: compass
rose on 4, 7, 9, 11, 13, 15, 17, 19, 25, 27; Jacques Langevin/Sygma/Corbis: 24tr; Vladislav Evgenievitch Lebedinski/Shutterstock: 20br, Frans Lemmen/
zefa/Corbis: 27b; Brandus Dan Lucian/Shutterstock: 25tl; Dylan Martinez/Reuters/Corbis: 20bl, Harry Maynard/Corbis: 6l; Natalia Sinjushina & Evgeniy
Meyke/Shutterstock: 11bl; Bruno Morandi/Corbis: 26bl; Hashim Pudiyapura/Shutterstock: 22tr, 23bl; Ryan Pyle/Corbis: 9tr; Altaf Qadri/epa/Corbis:
26br; Reuters/Corbis: 13b, 20cr; Galen Rowell/Corbis: 22cl, 23cl; Klaus Sailor/Shutterstock: 24bl; Antoine Serra/In Visu/Corbis: 18tr; Vishal Shah/
Shutterstock: 12bl; David Sutherland/Corbis: 9cl; Rob Swanson/Shutterstock: 22br; Adam Woolfitt/Corbis: 21br; Alison Wright/Corbis: 10bl; picture
research: info@picture-research.co.uk

Editor's Note: The maps in this book were created with the Miller projection.

Printed in the United States of America in Stevens Point, Wisconsin.
042011   006165

Table of Contents

Welcome to Southwest and Central Asia

The world is made up of five oceans and seven chunks of land called continents: North America, South America, Antarctica, Europe, Africa, Asia, and Australia.

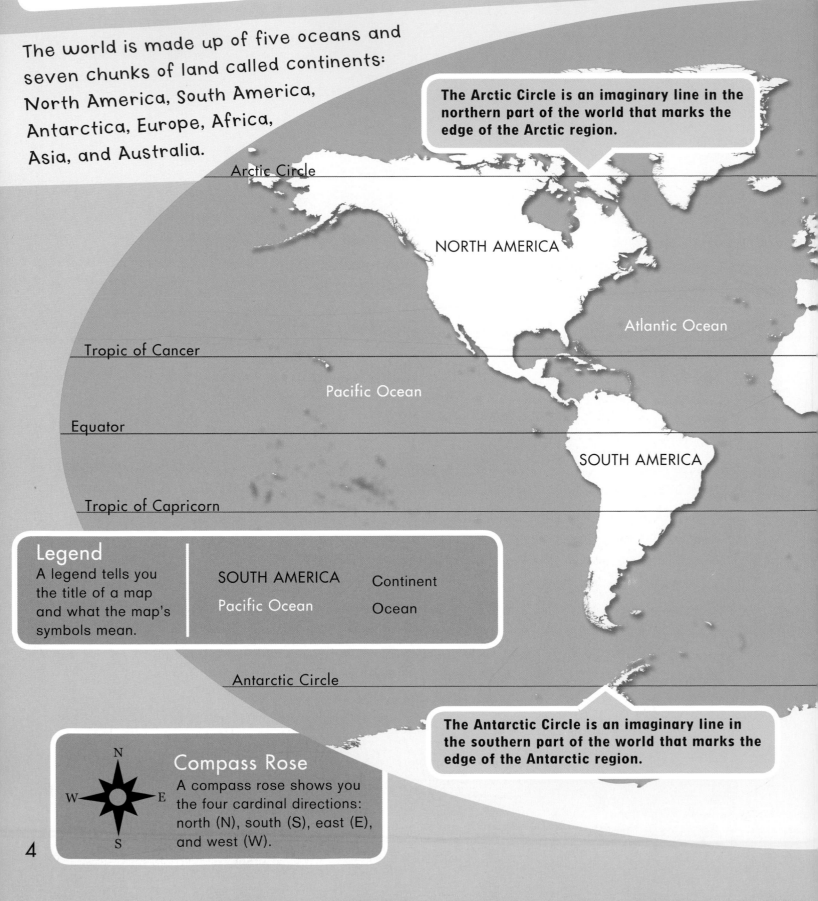

The **Arctic Circle** is an imaginary line in the northern part of the world that marks the edge of the Arctic region.

Arctic Circle

NORTH AMERICA

Atlantic Ocean

Tropic of Cancer

Pacific Ocean

Equator

SOUTH AMERICA

Tropic of Capricorn

Legend
A legend tells you the title of a map and what the map's symbols mean.

| SOUTH AMERICA | Continent |
| Pacific Ocean | Ocean |

Antarctic Circle

The **Antarctic Circle** is an imaginary line in the southern part of the world that marks the edge of the Antarctic region.

Compass Rose
A compass rose shows you the four cardinal directions: north (N), south (S), east (E), and west (W).

4

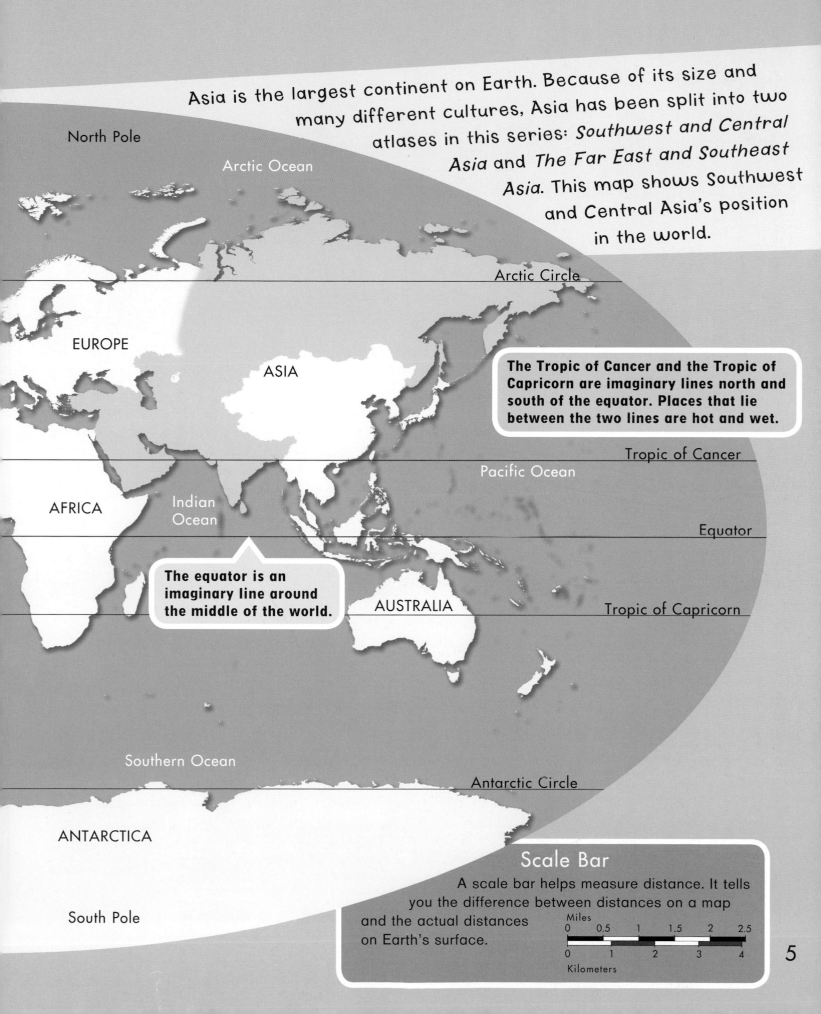

Asia is the largest continent on Earth. Because of its size and many different cultures, Asia has been split into two atlases in this series: *Southwest and Central Asia* and *The Far East and Southeast Asia*. This map shows Southwest and Central Asia's position in the world.

North Pole

Arctic Ocean

Arctic Circle

EUROPE

ASIA

The Tropic of Cancer and the Tropic of Capricorn are imaginary lines north and south of the equator. Places that lie between the two lines are hot and wet.

Tropic of Cancer

Pacific Ocean

AFRICA

Indian Ocean

Equator

The equator is an imaginary line around the middle of the world.

AUSTRALIA

Tropic of Capricorn

Southern Ocean

Antarctic Circle

ANTARCTICA

South Pole

Scale Bar

A scale bar helps measure distance. It tells you the difference between distances on a map and the actual distances on Earth's surface.

Miles
0   0.5   1   1.5   2   2.5

0   1   2   3   4
Kilometers

Countries

There are 32 countries in Southwest and Central Asia. The largest is Russia, part of which also lies on the continent of Europe. The smallest is the Maldives.

These 32 countries, added to those of the Far East and Southeast Asia, give the continent of Asia a grand total of 49 countries.

Some countries of Southwest Asia are often called the "Middle East." They include Cyprus, Iran, Iraq, Israel, Kuwait, Jordan, Lebanon, Oman, Qatar, Saudi Arabia, Syria, Turkey, United Arab Emirates, and Yemen. Two countries from the continent of Africa are also included in this group—Egypt and Sudan.

What's on the menu?

Cyprus – fried dough balls with honey

India – cauliflower and potato curry

Kazakhstan – smoked horsemeat sausages

Lebanon – grilled eggplant and garlic dip

Russia – beet soup

Saudi Arabia – spiced lamb with rice

Tajikistan – mutton (sheep) kebabs

Turkey – Turkish delight (a soft candy)

A man in a dishdasha

A woman in a sari

Getting dressed

In the hottest countries of Southwest and Central Asia, many people wear robes. Men in Saudi Arabia and neighboring countries wear a *dishdasha*, a long robe of white cotton. The color white helps reflect the warm rays of the sun. Women in India wear a long piece of cotton or silk cloth called a sari, which is wrapped loosely around the body.

AFGHANISTAN   ARMENIA   AZERBAIJAN

BAHRAIN   BANGLADESH   BHUTAN

CYPRUS   GEORGIA   INDIA

IRAN   IRAQ   ISRAEL

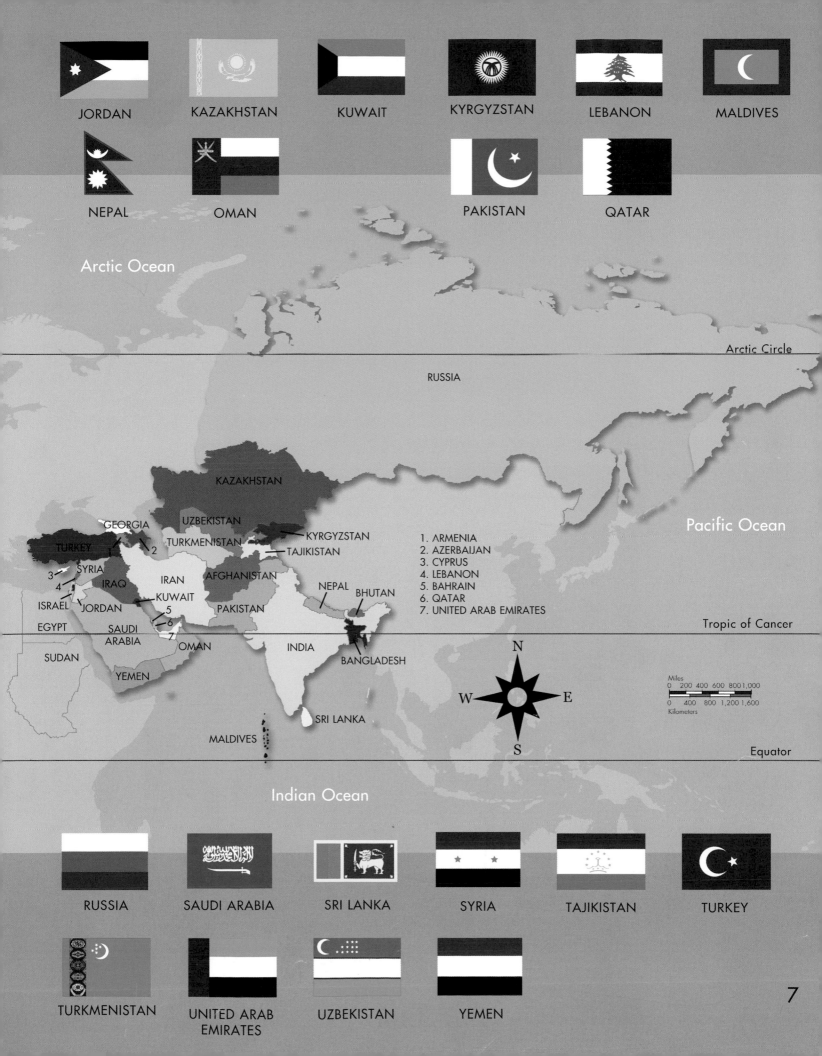

JORDAN

KAZAKHSTAN

KUWAIT

KYRGYZSTAN

LEBANON

MALDIVES

NEPAL

OMAN

PAKISTAN

QATAR

Arctic Ocean

Arctic Circle

RUSSIA

Pacific Ocean

KAZAKHSTAN

GEORGIA

UZBEKISTAN

TURKEY

TURKMENISTAN

KYRGYZSTAN

TAJIKISTAN

1. ARMENIA
2. AZERBAIJAN
3. CYPRUS
4. LEBANON
5. BAHRAIN
6. QATAR
7. UNITED ARAB EMIRATES

SYRIA

AFGHANISTAN

IRAN

NEPAL

BHUTAN

IRAQ

KUWAIT

ISRAEL

JORDAN

PAKISTAN

EGYPT

SAUDI
ARABIA

INDIA

BANGLADESH

SUDAN

OMAN

YEMEN

SRI LANKA

Tropic of Cancer

MALDIVES

N

W   E

S

Miles
0   200 400 600 800 1,000
0   400   800   1,200 1,600
Kilometers

Equator

Indian Ocean

RUSSIA

SAUDI ARABIA

SRI LANKA

SYRIA

TAJIKISTAN

TURKEY

TURKMENISTAN

UNITED ARAB
EMIRATES

UZBEKISTAN

YEMEN

7

Landforms

Much of Southwest and Central Asia is rugged and covered with mountains, plateaus, and highlands. The world's tallest mountains lie in this region.

But the region also has one of the world's largest stretches of low, flat land. The West Siberian Plain covers about one-third of Siberia. Siberia is the part of Russia that lies east of the Ural Mountains.

A lot of sand

The Rub' al Khali Desert is also known as the Empty Quarter. Deserts are not landforms, but the Rub' al Khali is an important part of Southwest Asia's landscape. It stretches across one-third of the Arabian Peninsula and is one of the largest sand deserts in the world.

The bare, sandy Rub' al Khali is very valuable land because it holds the world's largest amounts of oil.

The Himalayas

The Himalayas are the tallest mountains in the world. The mountain range was formed over millions of years and is still growing. The highest peak is Mount Everest. It stands 29,035 feet (8,856 meters) tall.

A view of the Himalayas

The salt swamp of Iran

In northern Iran lies a large, desert-like salt swamp called the Dasht-e Kavir. No one lives in this area. The ground is a lot like quicksand and is very dangerous to walk on.

The salty crust of Iran's Dasht-e Kavir

- Nearly all of Tajikistan—93 percent—is covered with mountains.
- The Ural Mountains form part of the boundary between Europe and Asia.
- The Deccan is a large plateau in India that covers most of the central and southern parts of the country.

Major Landforms

● place of interest   —— country boundary

🗻 mountain   ⛰ highland   🏔 plateau

Arctic Ocean

RUSSIA

S i b e r i a

Central Siberian Plateau

Verkhoyansk Mountains

East Siberian Uplands

Arctic Circle

West Siberian Plain

Ural Mountains

Sayan Mountains

Yablonovy Mountains

Stanovoy Mountains

Altay Mountains

Sea of Okhotsk

Kamchatka Peninsula

Caucasus Mountains

Black Sea

2

TAJIKISTAN

1

Dasht-e Kavir ●

Plateau of Iran

Mount Everest

Himalayas

Sea of Japan

Arabian Peninsula

INDIA

Tropic of Cancer

Red Sea

Rub' al Khali

Deccan

Pacific Ocean

Arabian Sea

Bay of Bengal

N

1. Mediterranean Sea
2. Caspian Sea

MALDIVES

W   E

S

Equator

Indian Ocean

The Maldives are a group of islands called atolls. An atoll is the tip of an extinct (dead) volcano that rises from the bottom of the ocean.

One of many atolls in the Maldives

9

Bodies of Water

Many rivers flow across Southwest and Central Asia. Three large, salty inland seas (the Aral Sea, the Caspian Sea, and the Dead Sea) also lie within the region.

Southwest and Central Asia share their borders with three oceans: the Arctic Ocean, the Pacific Ocean, and the Indian Ocean.

Dry riverbeds

A wadi is a dry riverbed. It contains water only during times of heavy rain. People in desert countries often live in wadis because there is always water just below the surface. However, wadis can be dangerous. When it rains, they flood suddenly, which can catch people off-guard.

When the rains come, this dry wadi may suddenly flood.

The Dead Sea

The Dead Sea is a very salty body of water in Southwest Asia. It is also the lowest point on Earth, lying 1,349 feet (411 meters) below sea level. The salt makes it possible for people to float easily on the water.

A swimmer floating on the Dead Sea

The Ganges River

The Ganges River is one of the world's most important rivers. It flows 1,557 miles (2,491 kilometers) from northeastern India to the Bay of Bengal. The Ganges is a holy river for followers of a religion called Hinduism. Hindus believe the Ganges is a goddess who forgives all sins and helps the dead reach heaven.

- Lake Baikal, in Central Asia, is the oldest, deepest freshwater lake on Earth. More than 330 rivers and streams flow into it. The lake's surface freezes for five or six months each year.
- The Aral Sea is turning into a desert. It has lost almost 75 percent of its water since 1960. Much of the water from incoming rivers is used for crops, cutting off the sea's water supply.

Arctic Ocean

Yenisey River

Lena River

Kolyma River

Arctic Circle

Ob River

Irtysh River

Aral Sea

Syr Darya River

Lake Balkhash

Lake Baikal

Sea of Okhotsk

Amur River

Sea of Japan

Black Sea

Amu Darya River

Lake Issykul

2

Tigris River

Euphrates River

1

Dead Sea

3

Indus River

Ganges River

Tropic of Cancer

Pacific Ocean

Red Sea

INDIA

N

Arabian Sea

Bay of Bengal

W   E

1. Mediterranean Sea
2. Caspian Sea
3. Persian Gulf

S

Equator

Indian Ocean

Lake Issykul is a huge lake. It lies in the crater of an old volcano. Water from melted snow in the nearby mountains feeds the lake. The water is so clear that you can see objects 40 feet (12 m) below the surface.

Lake Issykul is surrounded by mountains.

11

Climate

Climate is the average weather a place has from season to season, year to year. Rainfall and temperature play large parts in a region's climate.

Because the Southwest and Central Asia region stretches from above the Arctic Circle to the equator, it has a very wide range of climates.

Northernmost places have a polar climate, while southernmost places have a tropical climate.

In the Tropics

India, Bangladesh, and Sri Lanka lie in the Tropics. The climate is hot, but the countries' shores are cooled by ocean breezes. There is heavy rainfall when the monsoon winds blow in from the Indian Ocean.

A tropical beach in Sri Lanka

Mountain climate

High up in the tallest mountains of Southwest and Central Asia, it is cold all year. The snow and ice never melt. Ice fields form from snow that has become pressed and frozen into ice. In places, this pressing forms sharp "knives" of ice, like icicles pointing upward.

An ice field high in the mountains of Southwest Asia

Climate basics

A region's climate depends upon three major things: how close it is to the ocean, how high up it is, and how close it is to the equator. Areas along the ocean have milder climates than areas farther inland. The higher a region is, and the farther it is from the equator, the colder its temperature.

- June through September is the monsoon season in Southwest Asia. Places along the Indian Ocean may receive from 20 to 80 inches (51 to 203 centimeters) of rain during this time.

- In the far northern part of the continent, north of the Arctic Circle, the summer season lasts about a month. During this time, daylight can last almost 24 hours.

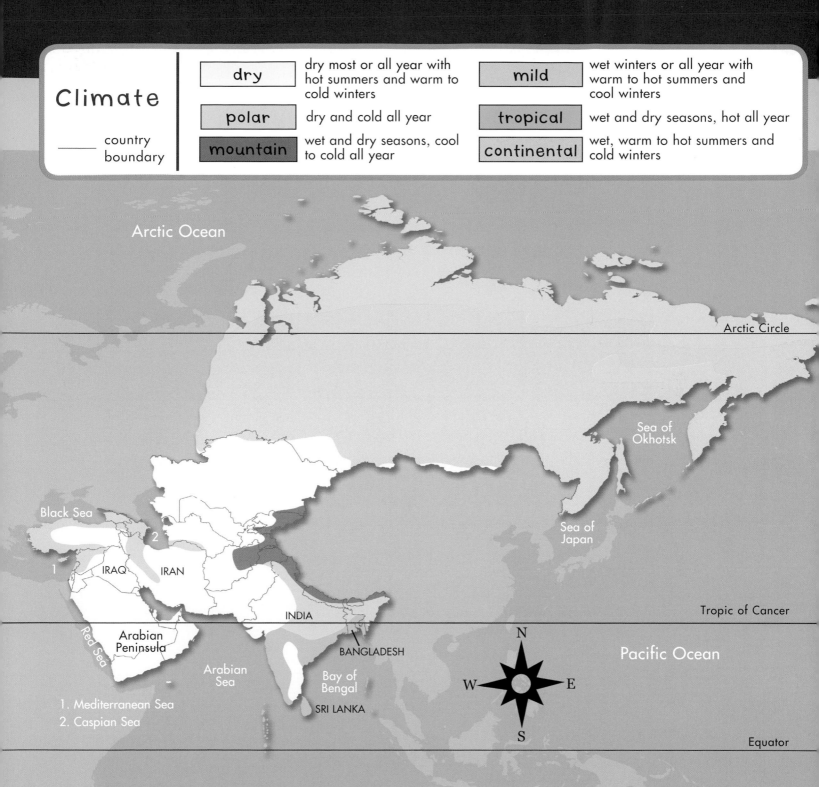

Climate

— country boundary

dry — dry most or all year with hot summers and warm to cold winters

polar — dry and cold all year

mountain — wet and dry seasons, cool to cold all year

mild — wet winters or all year with warm to hot summers and cool winters

tropical — wet and dry seasons, hot all year

continental — wet, warm to hot summers and cold winters

Arctic Ocean

Arctic Circle

Sea of Okhotsk

Black Sea

Sea of Japan

1

2

IRAQ   IRAN

INDIA

Tropic of Cancer

Red Sea

Arabian Peninsula

Arabian Sea

Bay of Bengal

BANGLADESH

Pacific Ocean

N
W   E
S

1. Mediterranean Sea
2. Caspian Sea

SRI LANKA

Equator

Indian Ocean

The shamal is a dry, dusty summer wind that blows over Iraq, Iran, and the Arabian Peninsula. It blows for about two months—often without stopping. It can cause terrible sandstorms.

It can be very difficult to see when the shamal is blowing.

Plants

Plants in Southwest and Central Asia are well-adapted to the region's many ecosystems, including deserts, forests, and mountains. An ecosystem is all of the living and nonliving things in a certain area. It includes plants, animals, soil, weather ... everything!

Some desert plants use drops of night dew for their water. The plants' leaves trap the water and keep it from evaporating (turning from a liquid to a gas) in the warmth of the day.

Plants that grow in cold places have bunched roots and leaves to hold any warmth and water tightly inside.

Some Plants of Southwest and Central Asia

Ecosystem	Plant	Description
desert	date palm	The date palm grows well in many parts of Southwest Asia. Its leaves are spiky, and its fruit is small and sticky.
desert	coffee bush	Coffee bush flowers are white and sweet-smelling. They last for a few days, then turn into coffee cherries months later.
forest	pine tree	Pines are a type of evergreen tree. The thick evergreen forests of northern Russia are the largest in the world. They cover an area the size of the United States.
forest	powder puff	The powder puff is a shrub with bright, long-lasting red or pink flowers. It grows well in India's warm, wet climate.
grassland	tulip	Tulips come in every color except blue and true black. Many people believe that the very first tulips came from Asia.
mountain	cedar tree	The cedar tree can be seen on the flag of Lebanon. Cedar trees grow on the low mountains of Lebanon, Syria, and Turkey.
rain forest	Indian lotus	The Indian lotus grows in the rain forest ecosystems of India and the surrounding countries. Lotus flowers may measure up to 8 inches (20 centimeters) across.
tundra	cushion plant	Cushion plants look like flat cushions, or round pillows, on the ground. The leaves are closely packed to protect the plant from wind, ice, and snow.

14

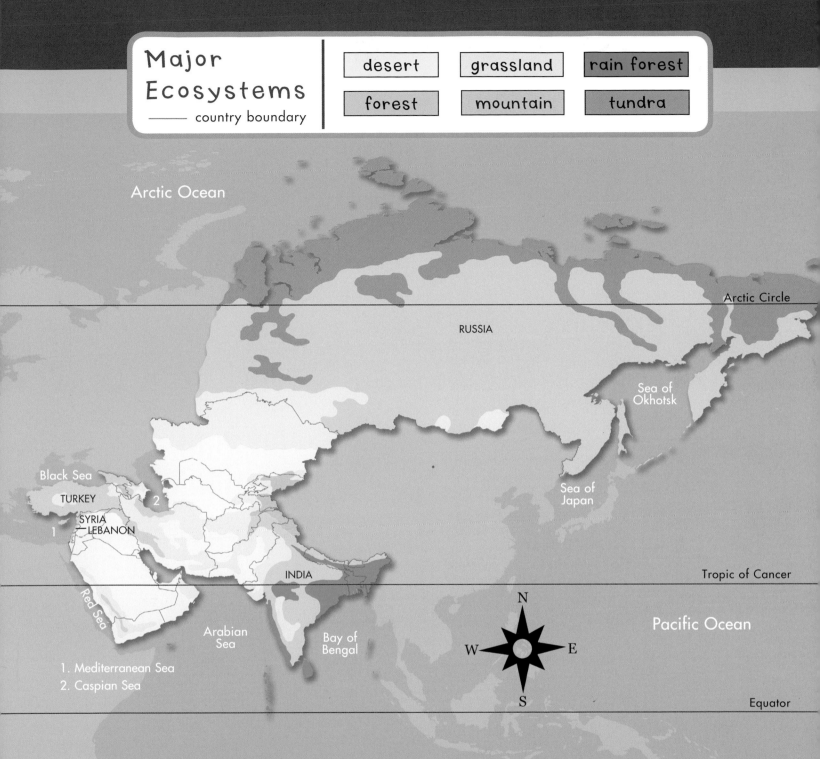

Major Ecosystems

—— country boundary

| desert | grassland | rain forest |
| forest | mountain | tundra |

Arctic Ocean

Arctic Circle

RUSSIA

Sea of Okhotsk

Black Sea

TURKEY

2

Sea of Japan

SYRIA
LEBANON

1

INDIA

Tropic of Cancer

Red Sea

Pacific Ocean

Arabian Sea

Bay of Bengal

N

W   E

1. Mediterranean Sea
2. Caspian Sea

S

Equator

Indian Ocean

Animals

The animals of Southwest and Central Asia have adapted, or changed, to survive in a wide range of ecosystems. An ecosystem is all of the living and nonliving things in a certain area.

Animals such as the yak and reindeer have shaggy coats to protect them in the cold mountains and tundra. Camels, cobras, and other animals that live in the dry desert can survive on little food and water.

Some Animals of Southwest and Central Asia

desert	Arabian camel	The Arabian (or dromedary) camel has one hump. The hump is filled with fat, not water. The camel uses the fat whenever there is little water or food.
	cobra	The cobra is a poisonous snake. It lives only in the desert regions of Asia.
	jerboa	Jerboas have hairs on the bottom of their feet that act as "snowshoes" in the deep desert sand.
	Arabian oryx	The Arabian oryx is a large antelope that can survive without water for long periods of time.
tundra	reindeer	The reindeer is a kind of deer that is well-adapted to living in the tundra. It has wide hooves so it can walk easily on soft snow and slippery ice.

forest	gaur	Gaurs are the largest species of wild cattle in the world. A full-grown male weighs about 1,000 pounds (450 kilograms).
	Siberian tiger	The Siberian tiger is the largest member of the cat family. It lives only in Central Asia.
	Asian elephant	The Asian elephant weighs less than the African elephant, has smaller ears, and has two bumps on its forehead.
	brown bear	Like humans, brown bears are omnivores. They feed on both plants and other animals.
mountain	yak	Yaks have large lungs. They help the animals breathe easier in the thin mountain air.
	lammergeier	The lammergeier is a large, eagle-like bird that lives high in the mountains. It is also called the bearded vulture.

16

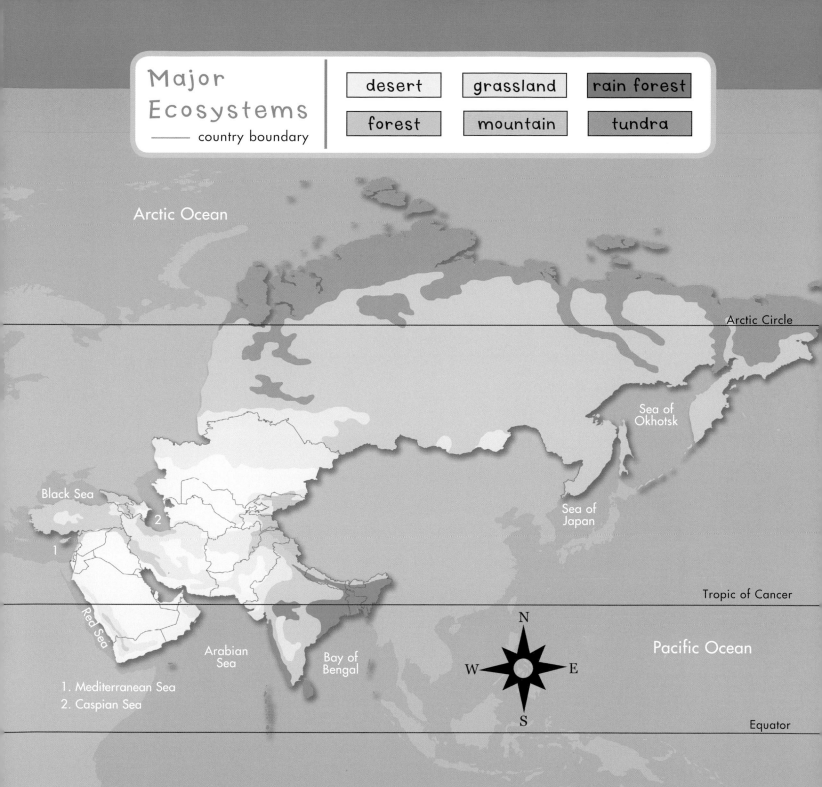

Major Ecosystems
—— country boundary

desert	grassland	rain forest
forest	mountain	tundra

Arctic Ocean

Arctic Circle

Sea of Okhotsk

Sea of Japan

Black Sea

2

1

Red Sea

Arabian Sea

Bay of Bengal

Tropic of Cancer

Pacific Ocean

1. Mediterranean Sea
2. Caspian Sea

N
W   E
S

Equator

Indian Ocean

Population

Much of Southwest and Central Asia is too dry, too mountainous, or too cold for people to live in.

For this reason, huge numbers of people live along the warm coasts and rivers of Pakistan, India, and Bangladesh. These areas average more than 2,000 people per square mile.

A crowded country

India is home to 1.1 billion people. It is the second-most populated country in the world (only China has more people). And it continues to grow each year. Eight of India's cities have more than 5 million people each.

Passengers crowd onto a train in Mumbai, India.

Living and working

Dubai, United Arab Emirates, is a fast-growing city. Its native population is so small, however, that 75 percent of the people living and working in Dubai have moved there from other countries around the world.

One big city

Mumbai, once called Bombay, is a busy port city. More than 12 million people live there. It is India's largest (and Southwest and Central Asia's largest) city. Many people come to Mumbai to find work in the textile, technology, and service industries. But with more people than jobs, not everyone can find work.

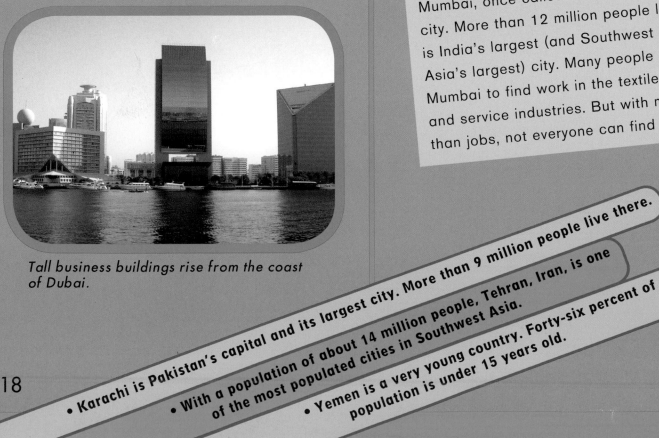

Tall business buildings rise from the coast of Dubai.

- Karachi is Pakistan's capital and its largest city. More than 9 million people live there.
- With a population of about 14 million people, Tehran, Iran, is one of the most populated cities in Southwest Asia.
- Yemen is a very young country. Forty-six percent of the population is under 15 years old.

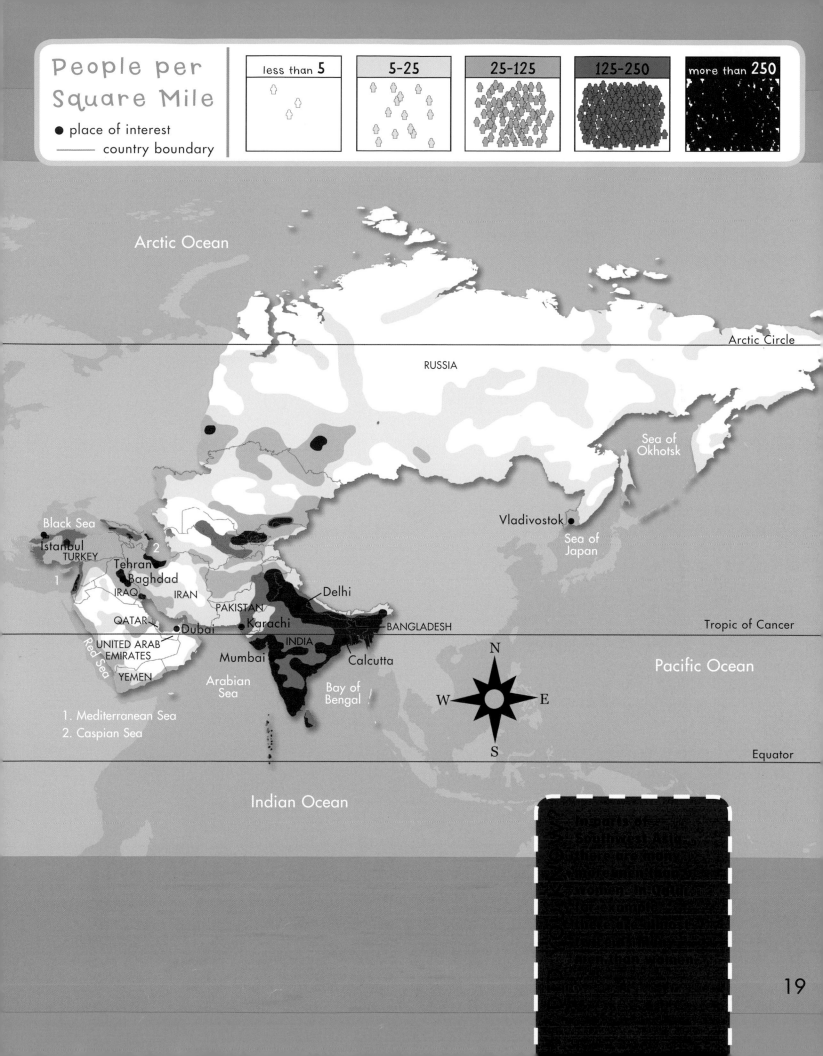

People per Square Mile

- ● place of interest
- —— country boundary

less than 5	5-25	25-125	125-250	more than 250

Arctic Ocean

Arctic Circle

RUSSIA

Sea of Okhotsk

Vladivostok ●

Sea of Japan

Black Sea

Istanbul ●
TURKEY

Tehran ●
Baghdad ●

1

2

IRAQ

IRAN

QATAR

Dubai ●

UNITED ARAB EMIRATES

Red Sea

YEMEN

PAKISTAN

Karachi ●

Delhi ●

BANGLADESH

Tropic of Cancer

Pacific Ocean

Mumbai ●

INDIA

Calcutta ●

Arabian Sea

Bay of Bengal

N

W · E

S

1. Mediterranean Sea
2. Caspian Sea

Indian Ocean

Equator

19

People and Customs

Asia has more people than any other continent in the world.

The many different languages, traditions, religions, foods, sports, and art forms of the people of Southwest and Central Asia make the region a colorful place to live.

A religious journey

The Hajj is the name of the journey that many Muslims make to Mecca, Saudi Arabia. The city is a holy site for Muslims. Every Muslim is supposed to try to make the Hajj at least once in his or her lifetime. Muslims are followers of the Islamic religion.

People gather to walk around the Kaaba, the holiest of all Islamic places.

Sports champions

Russia has produced many champion gymnasts. The sport of gymnastics focuses on a person's strength, balance, and body control. One of Russia's most successful gymnasts of all time is Svetlana Khorkina. During her career, she won five world championship titles on the uneven bars.

Svetlana Khorkina performs at the 2004 Olympic Games.

Snake tradition

The tradition of snake charming is slowly dying out. Many countries now have laws making it illegal to capture snakes. Snake charmers blow a horn to get a cobra to rise from a basket.

Snake charmers in Southwest Asia

The Bedouin

The Bedouin people live in the deserts of Southwest Asia. They stay on the move, driving their herds of sheep, goats, and camels from one grazing place to another. Today, many Bedouin earn extra money by selling handmade rugs, leather bags, and metal jewelry in the region's tourist centers.

A Bedouin man sets up his tent home.

Holy cows

People who practice the Hindu religion consider cows holy. In India, where most people are Hindu, cows are allowed to roam freely in the cities. Surprisingly, the cows always look calm and wise, whatever noisy traffic is around.

Cows rest in a busy Indian street.

Turkish baths

Turkish baths, known locally as *hamam*, are very old. Like the ancient Roman baths, the hamam are a place where friends can meet to chat and relax.

Men relax on a marble gobek tasi, *or "belly stone," at a Turkish bath.*

Postcard Places

Sand dunes in Dubai

The high sand dunes of Dubai, United Arab Emirates, are a great place to go racing, roaring, slipping, and sliding in an SUV (sport-utility vehicle).

On top of the world

People from all over the world come to the Himalayan mountains to climb the world's highest peak, Mount Everest.

Jerusalem

Jerusalem, Israel, is a holy city for the people of three major religions: Christians, Jews, and Muslims. The golden Dome of the Rock is a famous city landmark.

- • Ephesus
- • Jerusalem
- • Dubai
- Agra
- Himalayas
- • Mount Everest
- • SRI LANKA

22

The Taj Mahal is a beautiful white marble building in Agra, India. An emporer had it built in the 1600s as a memorial to his favorite wife.

Taj Mahal

Thyangboche Monastery lies in the Himalayas, in the shadow of Mount Everest. It is home to about 35 Buddhist monks.

Mountain monastery

Visit Turkey

Sigiriya

Sigiriya stands in the center of Sri Lanka, high above the surrounding plain. It was formed by hot liquid rock that cooled and hardened in the mouth of a volcano. On top of Sigiriya are the ruins of a palace built in the 5th century.

The ancient ruins of Ephesus, Turkey, include a huge amphitheater that could seat 24,000 people. It was first used for open-air plays. In later times, Roman gladiators (fighters) battled on the stage.

Growing and Making

Most of the world's oil is found in Southwest and Central Asia. Leading oil producers include Saudi Arabia, Iran, Iraq, Kuwait, United Arab Emirates, Russia, Qatar, Kazakhstan, and India.

The southwest region's warm, dry climate is perfect for growing fruits and spices.

Mining is the top industry in Central Asia, where large supplies of metal and coal lie deep beneath the ground.

Drilling for oil

Oil is a black or dark brown liquid trapped in layers of rock deep underground. Oil forms naturally, over millions of years, from rotten plants. Saudi Arabia is the world's leading oil producer. It sends more than 90 percent of its oil to other countries.

A huge oil refinery in Saudi Arabia

Carpet making

The oldest "knotted" carpet was found in the frozen tomb of a Persian chief who lived 2,400 years ago. Persia, now called Iran, is still the center of the world's carpet-making industry.

Persian carpets are beautiful works of art.

At the movies

"Bollywood" is a nickname given to the huge film industry in Mumbai, India. The name comes from adding "Bombay" (Mumbai's former name) and "Hollywood." Bollywood makes nearly 1,000 movies each year—about three a day!

- The hot, wet climate of Bangladesh is perfect for growing jute. Jute is a long, strong, natural fiber that comes from the thick bark of the jute plant. It is used to make sacks and rope.

- Iran exports more dates than any other country in the world. Dates are the small, reddish-brown, sticky fruit of the date palm tree.

- The largest industry in Tajikistan is aluminum, followed by agriculture.

Major Natural Resources, Land Use, and Industry

● place of interest
—— country boundary

Technology

Manufacturing

Tourism

Natural Gas

Oil

Mining
diamonds
metal
gold
coal

Farming
cotton
jute
dates
fruit
nuts
spices

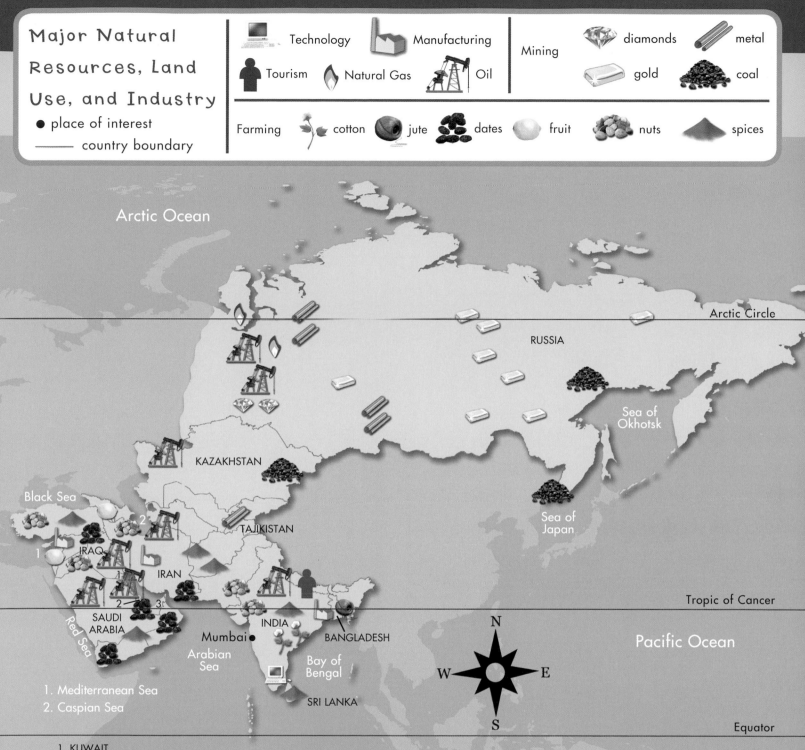

Arctic Ocean

Arctic Circle

RUSSIA

KAZAKHSTAN

Sea of Okhotsk

Black Sea

2

TAJIKISTAN

Sea of Japan

IRAQ

1

IRAN

1

Tropic of Cancer

2   3

SAUDI ARABIA

INDIA

Mumbai ●

Red Sea

Arabian Sea

BANGLADESH

Pacific Ocean

Bay of Bengal

N

W   E

S

1. Mediterranean Sea
2. Caspian Sea

SRI LANKA

Equator

1. KUWAIT
2. QATAR
3. UNITED ARAB EMIRATES

Indian Ocean

A spice is a dried seed, fruit, or other plant part. It is crushed into a powder and used to add flavor to food. Cinnamon, cloves, and pepper are some of the spices grown in Asia. Sri Lanka is one of the largest cinnamon exporters in the world.

Fresh spices for sale at a marketplace in Southwest Asia

25

Transportation

Transportation by land in Southwest and Central Asia can be a challenge. The region's mountains, deserts, and climate extremes make it hard to get around.

Trains, buses, and trucks are the most common methods of transportation. Air travel is becoming more common, too.

Ships carry goods to and from port cities on the Indian Ocean.

Trans-Siberian Railway

The Trans-Siberian Railway takes people across Russia, from Moscow to Vladivostok—a journey of 7,500 miles (12,000 kilometers). It took workers more than 30 years to build the railroad. They laid track across many rivers, lakes, and swamps and blasted through miles of frozen ground.

The Trans-Siberian train takes 14 days to travel across Russia.

Mountain railways

India has a number of "Hill Railways." The railways were built long ago to help people escape from the hot low-lying cities to the cool hillside towns. In some towns, trains stop on the main street so passengers can easily hop off and buy goods.

Railways are one way of transporting people and goods in the Indian hills.

On the water

Some of the land in southwestern India lies below sea level. It is crisscrossed by rivers, canals, lakes, lagoons, and tiny streams. In earlier times, barge-like boats (called houseboats) were used to carry rice from place to place. Today the boats are more often used by tourists.

Houseboats in southwestern India

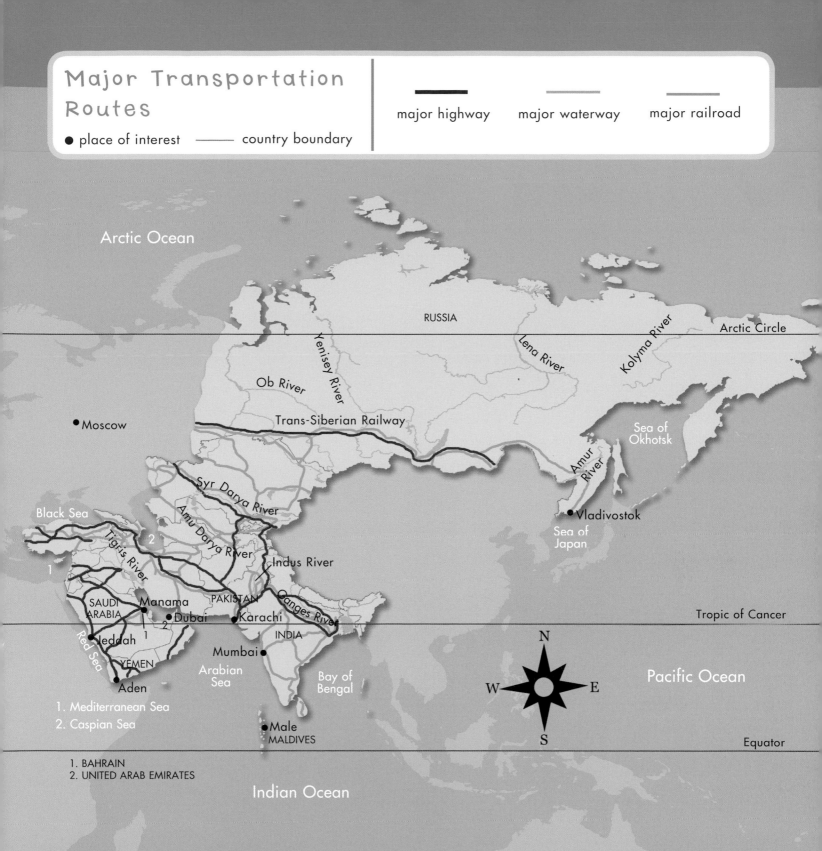

Major Transportation Routes

● place of interest ——— country boundary

—— major highway ——— major waterway ——— major railroad

Arctic Ocean

RUSSIA

Arctic Circle

Yenisey River

Lena River

Kolyma River

Ob River

Trans-Siberian Railway

Sea of Okhotsk

Amur River

Moscow

●Vladivostok

Sea of Japan

Syr Darya River

Black Sea

Amu Darya River

Tigris River

Indus River

2

1

SAUDI ARABIA

Manama ●

● Dubai

PAKISTAN

Ganges River

Karachi ●

INDIA

Tropic of Cancer

1

2

Jeddah ●

Red Sea

YEMEN

Mumbai ●

Arabian Sea

Bay of Bengal

Pacific Ocean

Aden ●

1. Mediterranean Sea
2. Caspian Sea

●Male
MALDIVES

N
W   E
S

Equator

1. BAHRAIN
2. UNITED ARAB EMIRATES

Indian Ocean

Camels are known as "ships of the desert" because they are the perfect pack animals. They are often able to carry 300 pounds (135 kilograms) and can journey for up to two weeks in the hot desert without food or water.

A camel train crosses a desert in southwestern Asia.

Journey Up Mount Everest

It is early in the morning. The climbers are leaving the base camp at the foot of the Himalayan mountains. They are hoping to climb Mount Everest, the highest mountaintop (peak) in the world. Base camp is more than 16,000 feet (4,880 meters) up the slope. But there are still four more camps and days of climbing ahead.

The temperature is already well below zero. It will get colder the higher the team climbs. The climbers will soon start to feel out of breath. Some of them carry bottles of oxygen to help them breathe easier.

The first challenge is the Khumbu Icefall. This area of cracked ice is very dangerous. The climbers need ropes and ladders to bridge the cracks. Avalanches (fast-moving masses of snow) could sweep the climbers away at any time.

Once past the Khumbu Icefall, the team moves to Camp 2 through a glacier valley. Here it is hot. The wind is calm, and the sun reflects off the ice with dazzling heat.

Camp 3 and Camp 4 are farther up. Both lie on the far side of walls of ice. Ropes and climbing hooks are needed to get a foothold on the ice.

From Camp 4, the climbers make their final climb to the peak. They start out long before sunrise.

On a platform of rock known as "The Balcony," the team rests before climbing a tall wall of snow and rock. They must go up this using a rope, one at a time.

The view from the top of Mount Everest is breathtaking. The climbers take a few photos. But they don't stay too long. The climb down will take three more days, and it will be just as dangerous.

Mount Everest

Measured from the peak to sea level, Mount Everest stands 29,035 feet (8,856 m) high. The mountain is on the border between Nepal and China. Mount Everest has two main climbing routes—the southeast ridge from Nepal and the northeast ridge from China. Of these two main routes, the southeast ridge is easier to climb.

Southwest and Central Asia At-a-Glance

Continent size: Asia, as a whole, is the largest of Earth's seven continents

Number of countries: 32 in the region, 49 total in Asia; Russia and Turkey lie in two continents—Europe and Asia

Major languages:
- Arabic
- Bengali
- English
- Greek
- Hebrew
- Hindi
- Persian
- Russian
- Turkish

Total population: 1.9 billion in the region, 4 billion total in Asia (2007 estimate)

Largest country (land size): Russia

Most populated country: India

Most populated city: Mumbai, India

Climate: mostly dry in Southwest Asia, with a mild climate around the Black Sea and the Mediterranean Sea; continental (wet, warm to hot summers and cold winters) in the East; dry and cold all year in the far North; dry in the southeastern and southwestern regions; cool to cold in the mountains

Highest point: Mount Everest, Nepal/China, 29,035 feet (8,856 meters)

Lowest point: Dead Sea, Israel/Jordan, 1,349 feet (411 m) below sea level

Longest river: Ob-Irtysh River

Largest body of water: Caspian Sea

Largest desert: Rub' al Khali Desert

Major agricultural products:
- citrus fruits
- cotton
- dates
- goats
- grapes
- jute
- olives
- peanuts
- rice
- sheep
- spices
- wheat

Major industries:
- agriculture
- construction
- mining
- manufacturing (clothing, chemicals, food and beverage, cement, steel, and electronic equipment)

Natural resources:
- aluminum
- coal
- copper
- gold
- natural gas
- nickel
- oil
- phosphate
- steel

Glossary

body of water – a mass of water that is in one area; such as a river, lake, or ocean

boundary – a line that shows the border of a country, state, or other land area

canal – a waterway dug across land

climate – the average weather a place has from season to season, year to year

compass rose – a symbol used to show direction on a map

continent – one of seven large land masses on Earth, including Africa, Antarctica, Asia, Australia, Europe, North America, and South America

crops – plants that are grown in large amounts and are used for food or income

desert – a hot or cold, very dry area that has few plants growing on it

dune – a hill of sand piled up by the wind

ecosystem – all of the living and nonliving things in a certain area, including plants, animals, soil, and weather

equator – an imaginary line around Earth; it divides the northern and southern hemispheres

export – to send goods to another country to be sold or traded

forest – land covered by trees and plants

glacier – a huge, slow-moving mass of ice

grassland – land covered mostly with grass

highland – high or hilly land

island – land that is completely surrounded by water

lagoon – a shallow body of water that lies near or is connected to a larger body of water

lake – a body of water that is completely surrounded by land

landform – a natural feature on Earth's surface

legend – the part of a map that explains the meaning of the map's symbols

monsoon – a strong wind that blows across southern Asia and the Indian Ocean

mountain – a mass of land that rises high above the land that surrounds it

natural resources – materials such as water, trees, and minerals that are found in nature

North Pole – the northern-most point on Earth

ocean – the large body of saltwater that covers most of Earth's surface

oxygen – a gas in air that plants and animals need to live

peninsula – a body of land that is surrounded by water on three sides

plateau – a large, flat, and often rocky area of land that is higher than the surrounding land

population – the total number of people who live in one area

port – a place where ships can load or unload cargo (goods or people)

rain forest – a thick forest that receives a lot of rain year-round

river – a large stream of water that empties into a lake, ocean, or other river

scale – the size of a map or model compared to the actual size of things they stand for

South Pole – the southern-most point on Earth

species – groups of animals or plants that have many things in common

temperature – how hot or cold something is

tundra – land with no trees that lies in the arctic regions

valley – a low place between mountains or hills

31

Index

On the Web

FactHound offers a safe, fun way to find Web sites related to topics in this book. All of the sites on FactHound have been researched by our staff.

1. Visit *www.facthound.com*
2. Type in this special code: 1404838848
3. Click on the FETCH IT button.

Your trusty FactHound will fetch the best sites for you!

Look for all of the books in the Picture Window Books World Atlases series: